Women's Code for
Self Defence

By the same author

COMPREHENSIVE SELF DEFENCE
SELF DEFENCE BY JUDO
THE JUDO INSTRUCTOR

WARNING!
ALL THE ACTIONS DESCRIBED IN THIS BOOK
ARE POTENTIALLY DANGEROUS AND SHOULD
THEREFORE BE PRACTISED WITH CAUTION.

Women's Code for
Self Defence

Brigadier 'Mike' Harvey CBE MC

3rd dan JUDO   1st dan AIKIDO

former Commandant of the
Army School of Physical Training

Consultant in Restraint and Arrest Systems
to the Army and Police

Kaye & Ward · Kingswood

Photographs by Peter C. Clark
Actions modelled by Miss Susan Morley and Mr. T. M. Davis

Contents

Self defence for women and girls **6**

One hand at the throat (standing) **12**

Two hands at the throat **18**

Both elbows held from the front **33**

Hand on the chest/breast **37**

Both wrists held from the front **41**

One wrist held from the front **47**

Enveloped over the arms from the front **49**

Enveloped under the arms from the front **51**

Two hands around the throat from the rear **54**

Arm encircles the throat from the rear **58**

Both arms encircled from the rear **61**

Enveloped from the rear **63**

Encircled under the arms from the rear **65**

Both wrists held from the rear **67**

Held by the hair from the rear **71**

Held down on the ground – attacker in astride position **73**

Held on the ground in the 'rape' position **76**

Self defence for women and girls

The aim of this book is to present simple and effective self defence for women and girls without the need for formal Martial Arts training. When used in conjunction with the practical precautionary contingency measures recommended a significant level of self protection is achieved.

Women in general have little time or opportunity to undergo formal training in the Martial Arts. This does not mean that one need not practise! Efficient and effective disciplined response in a situation of high stress can only be developed by repetitive exercises. When this is concentrated onto the movements advocated, a high level of ability should result. Clearly, if a grounding in any Martial Art is available it should be undertaken. It will enhance posture, balance, maximum efficient use of the body mechanism, the ability to concentrate full striking power precisely onto vulnerable targets and more important, will develop self confidence.

'Restraint and Arrest' systems developed and taught by the author and favoured by the Security Forces and Law Enforcement Agencies are rightly constrained by the critical requirement to apply MINIMUM FORCE consistent with achieving the immediate aim. Here only specialised training within an eclectic system from the whole spectrum of the Martial Arts can provide a comprehensive variety of Restraint and Arrest techniques with which to deal with those unarmed, or armed with offensive weapons. This provides a system which controls the level of violence in a humane way consistent with the level of resistance encountered. This is clearly beyond the scope and aims of this book. However, the constraints of 'minimum force' do not apply to the present reader nor does the need to effect unaided a professional arrest!

Methods purposely barred from the 'sports' because of their inherent danger to the players are included because of their sheer effectiveness. Techniques of old Ju-Jitsu from the samurai's Kumiuchi methods, excluded by the rules in the 'sports' are reinstated to meet the modern contingencies in an age devoid of chivalry.

The aim of the contingency plans and techniques described are to outline simple preventive measures and effective release techniques. These presenting the opportunity to RUN and raise the alarm! NEVER stay to follow up the initial shock effected – however seemingly successful!

Do not be afraid to use your voice to the best advantage! Always carry a whistle. In your home have an 'alarm tapping' system on the wall or plumbing with your neighbour. In extreme situations a heavy object thrown through the window will invariably bring instant investigation and support. Moreover stealth and the element of surprise, and therefore initiative on which the intruder relies, is compromised.

An assailant relies on opportunity, stealth and surprise. By taking maximum practicable precautions opportunity may be significantly reduced. A well laid plan can be rudely disrupted by surprise offensive action and the attacker's initiative lost! Stealth can readily be compromised by noise thereby imposing a hasty retreat.

What can sensibly be done? Obviously it is a matter of common sense never to knowingly place yourself in an avoidable vulnerable position. Here are some guidelines.

NEVER Walk alone at night unless it is totally unavoidable. Then select well lit routes avoiding short cuts through 'risk areas'. (Alleyways, parks, car parks, waste ground, subways, etc.)

NEVER Walk close to buildings past unlit doorways and alleyways, keep well out from the buildings to avoid being 'jumped'.

NEVER Pass through a subway until you can utilise an escort of other people passing that way.

NEVER Walk with both hands thrust into your pockets.

NEVER Carry heavy bags in both hands at the same time.

NEVER Walk along in a daydream, try and remain alert to your immediate surroundings. If you must pass through a 'risk area' plan what you would do at any point of contact and what precautionary measures you might take in selection of escape routes or choice of 'improvised weapons', explained below, are to hand. Your whistle should be instantly accessible. Don't be afraid to blow it in a false alarm – be SAFE.

NEVER Use provocation which could needlessly escalate an 'armed threat' into an 'armed attack'. Retention of property is of trivial consequence to loss of life! An 'attack' is entirely another matter calling for 'maximum effective resistance'!

NEVER Stay to follow up your surprise action – however apparently successful – your primary objective is to escape!

NEVER Wait at an isolated, unlit bus stop. Time your arrival there to coincide with others at the stop. If it is late, dark and isolated – be escorted.

NEVER Open your door to a stranger after dark, or let in a 'tradesman' without a prior appointment!

NEVER Fail to draw the curtains after dark if in the house alone!

The following 'weapons' have been used to good effect in the past, and are an available 'armoury' in the handbag pocket or in the home. Remember however, that the Law demands that items must NOT be carried for the sole purpose of Self-Defence! Therefore, coins, combs, shoes and umbrellas are items one could reasonably be expected to carry.

WEIGHTS
A weight in the hand will add momentum and considerable impact when striking vulnerable targets. Use a handful of small coins, cigarette lighter or bunch of keys.

COMB
A comb can be used to effect in slashing and scratching at the eyes and face. (Avoidance of such marking and scratching is important to the assailant in the preservation of identity. It will discourage all but the most resolute).

SHOE
The high heeled shoe is a formidable weapon in a determined hand. The focus of force onto a small target coupled with full power and momentum, is the applied fundamental principle of blows struck in Karate and Judo (Atemi-waza), with devastating effect!

UMBRELLA
An umbrella used in thrusting to the body and raking to the face can be most effective. (Never to be used in ineffective striking actions which have no potential power and can be easily avoided).

Items in the kitchen and home which come readily to hand in an emergency, have also been used to effect.

PEPPER
Pepper thrown into the face is an effective deterrent, as are the contents of various aerosol sprays.

EARTH
Earth, sand or small change thrown unexpectedly into the face will facilitate a good diversion before striking or RUNNING to raise the alarm.

All these methods can be used in conjunction with the self defence techniques which follow, if only to gain a momentary advantage when the assailant flinches. A combination of rapidly applied measures will have a much greater chance of success than an isolated single action. Always avoid a futile trial of strength where practicable and strike hard at a vulnerable target. For example, do not grip the wrists of the assailant unless it is required in the technique. Instead, strike with maximum force any and every exposed target!

What are the best targets? The points of KYUSHO, vulnerable points distilled from centuries of practical experience in the Martial Arts, provide the best guidelines on where to strike the physiologically weak points of the human frame and it's nerve centres. All blows struck are made in a whipping action with the hand or foot instantly withdrawn. If you can, a local use of the arms or leg should be avoided. The main muscle groups of the trunk and body weight should lead the action.

The vulnerable points within the scope of this pamphlet are as follows:

a. Eyes
b. The nose
c. Under the nose (junction of the upper lip and nose)
d. Each side of the 'Adams apple'
e. Solar plexus
f. Groin
g. The shin
h. Below the ears on the neck
i. Temples
j. The point and sides of the chin

As stressed previously, where practicable, attack more than one target in rapid and continuous succession. This will significantly reduce anticipation.

Remember this book is constrained by the aim to teach only what is practical and within the capabilities of a girl or woman.

To gain the greatest effect when striking, focus maximum force onto as small a target area as possible. This can be achieved by using the following 'natural weapons' as illustrated.

The finger tips
The edge of the hand
The one knuckle punch
The heel of the palm
The elbow
The knee
The foot
The head
The 'weighted' fist

Here again the attack forms are constrained by the limited aim of the book. *It is better by far to have a limited range of defences which you can 'do well', than a comprehensive 'knowledge'.*

The contingency actions described in this book cover the following situations.

1. One Hand at the Throat (Standing)
    Method 1a
    Method 1b

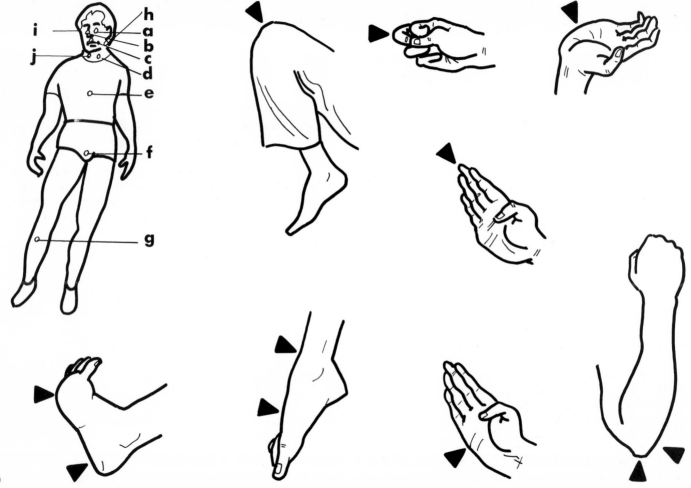

2. Two Hands at the Throat
   Method 2a
   Method 2b
   Method 2c
   Method 2d
   Method 2e
3. Both Elbows Held from the Front
4. Hand on the Chest/Breast
5. Both Wrists Held from the Front
   Method 5a
   Method 5b
6. One Wrist Held from the Front
   Method 6a
   Method 6b
7. Enveloped Over the Arms from the Front
8. Enveloped Under the Arms from the Front
9. Two Hands around the Throat from the Rear
10. Arm Encircling the Throat from the Rear
11. Both Arms Encircled from the Rear
12. Enveloped from the Rear
13. Encircled Under the Arms from the Rear
14. Both Wrists Held from the Rear
15. Held by the Hair from the Rear
16. Held Down on the Ground
17. Held Down in the 'Rape' position.

For the purpose of simplicity all techniques are described against a right handed assailant.

After practice, you should be able to effect total SURPRISE by moving quickly and precisely without preparatory actions which telegraph your intentions to the assailant. You may only need such protection once in a lifetime, but it is the one time that it may really count!

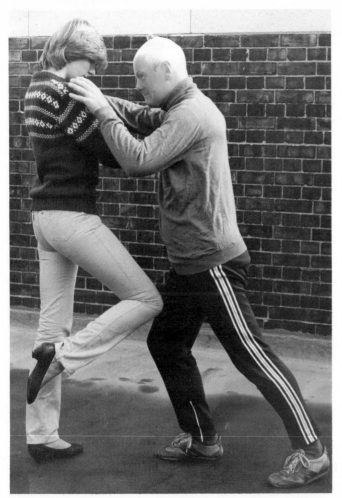

Fig. 1

One hand at the throat (standing)

1a.

In the process of closing in an attack, you are gripped by the attacker at the throat with his right hand (Fig. 1). Before the left hand takes hold or strikes – immediately –

(1) Kick the assailant in the groin with your right foot or knee (distance will dictate).

(2) At the same time grasp the hand at your throat with both hands on the base of the hand with your thumbs underneath (Fig. 2) – turn to your right

Fig. 2

Fig. 3

Fig. 4

One hand at
the throat
(standing)

withdrawing your right foot from the kick you have
just made, rotating the assailants arm inwards as hard
as you can. Without pause, pass your left elbow above
the assailants arm – throw your weight downwards
onto the elbow joint, keeping his captured hand up
(Fig. 3). Keep turning to the right. The assailant will
fall (Fig. 4) – RUN.

Fig. 5

Fig. 6

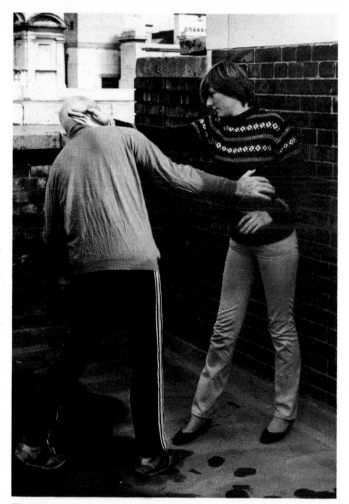

Fig. 7

1b.

You are pinned to the wall by the assailants right hand at your throat. This would probably be more likely than 1a above.

(1) Immediately drive the knee upwards against his groin (Fig. 5).

(2) and without pause, drive the heel of your right palm against the inside of the assailants wrist (Fig. 6), which will break or relieve the grip.

(3) Let your right hand continue back over your left shoulder as you turn from the waist to the left – your right elbow should now be pointing forward. Bring your right hand back without pause in a chopping action as hard as you can (reinforced by turning your shoulders to the front) (Fig. 7) striking the assailant on the neck below the right ear.

(4) – if necessary – butt the assailant in the face with the front of your head.

17

Two hands at the throat

2a.
Your assailant pins you to the wall with both hands at your throat.
(1) As he takes this grip, take a deep breath and cup your hands together (but do not interlace the fingers) then swing your arms upwards between his arms as fast and as high as you can (Fig. 8) – breaking his hold (Fig. 9).

Fig. 8

Fig. 9

Two hands at
the throat

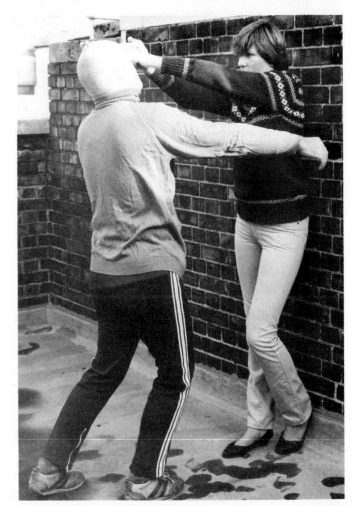

20 (2) – without pause, bring your cupped hands down
onto the bridge of his nose (Fig. 10).

Fig. 10

Fig. 11

(3) Drive your knee hard into the groin (Fig. 11) –
RUN.

Fig. 12

2b.
The assailant takes the two handed hold on the throat.
(1) Grasp both of his elbows, one in each hand, and pull
downwards hard (Fig. 12) – immediately without
pause, as it draws him forward off balance –

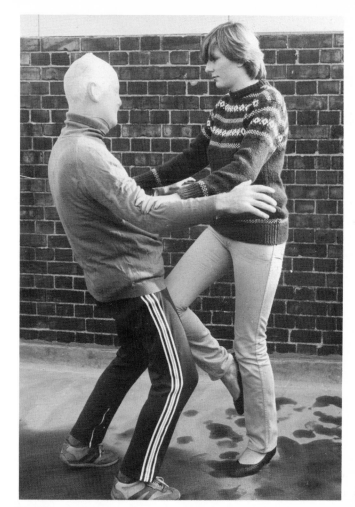

(2) Drive the knee as hard as you can against his groin (Fig. 13).
(3) Drive your hand upwards, the heel palm striking his chin, and if necessary, continue the hands movement upwards driving the fingers into the eyes – RUN.

Fig. 13

2c.
The assailant takes the two handed hold on your throat
as before.
(1) Drive the heel palm hard up against his chin in a
violent blow (Fig. 14.) –

24

Fig. 14

Fig. 15

(2) **Without pause (Fig. 15) turn your hand and drive
the ulna border as hard as you can upwards to the**

25

26

Fig. 16

junction of the nose and upper lip (Fig. 16).

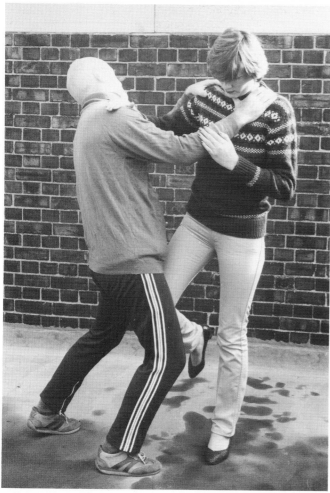

Fig. 17

(3) As you break free – drive the knee hard against his
groin (Fig. 17) – RUN.

27

2d.

The assailant grasps you by the throat with two hands in a free standing position, this time away from the wall or obstacle.

(1) Drive the knee into the groin and at the same time pass your right hand over the assailant's left arm grasping his right wrist (Fig. 18). Pass your left hand below the assailants right arm grasping his left wrist, raising your left elbow up under his right elbow joint.

28

Fig. 18

(2) Without pause, withdraw your right foot a full pace
to the rear turning your body to the right bending
forward from the waist (Fig. 19).
(3) The combined action when done with your full
power and momentum will throw the assailant
headlong – RUN.

29

Fig. 19

2e.
The assailant has you pinned to the ground and has
two hands at your throat. (See also movements 16 and
17).
(1) Drive your cupped hands upward as you did before
between his arms and strike his nose with full force
(Fig. 20).

Fig. 20

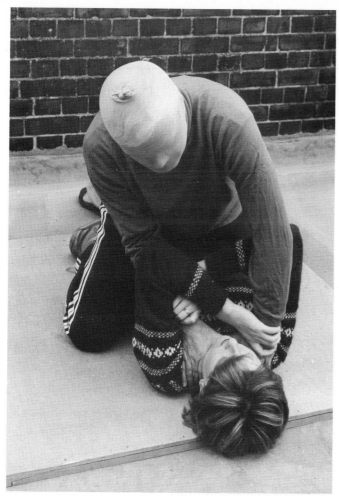

Fig. 21

(2) Immediately, before he involuntarily moves his arms, place your hands and arms against his arms as previously described in 2d(1) above (Fig. 21), and with the reinforced momentum, using your drawn up right foot against the floor and twisting your body to the left, roll your assailant off to the left by locking his left elbow (Fig. 22).

This should be practiced to the left and right.

Get up and – RUN.

31

Fig. 22

Both elbows held from the front

3.
The assailant grasps you by both elbows from the front to force you backwards or down.
(1) Bring your left arm over his right wrist in an outward circle and grasp the back of your left hand with your right hand (Fig. 23).
(2) Drive your knee into his groin at the same time.

33

Fig. 23

(3) Pull down as hard as you can on his right wrist locking it against your arm (Fig. 24), and adding momentum by dropping onto your right knee, draw him down onto his right knee.

Fig. 24

Fig. 25

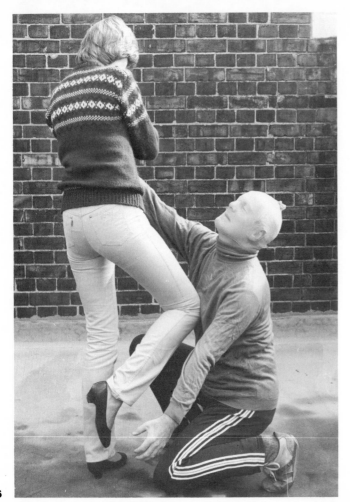

Fig. 26

(4) Without pause, rise up (Fig. 25) and bringing your right leg forward in a brisk sweeping movement, kick him hard in the groin or solar plexus (Fig. 26) – RUN.

This method can be applied to either wrist when grasped by two hands, one on each elbow, or singularly against a one-handed grip at the elbow.

36

Fig. 27

Hand on the chest/breast

4.

Your assailant places a hand on your breast.
(1) Place your own hands one above the other on the back of his hand (Fig. 27), pulling his hand between your breasts and pressing hard to retain it there, act as follows.

Fig. 28

Fig. 29

(2) Step back your right foot dropping onto the knee and bending forward from the waist (Fig. 28). This will lock his wrist in a similar manner to the preceeding lock forcing it back, the back of the hand towards his elbow.

(3) Without pause, recover to the standing position driving your knee or foot hard into his groin, or solar plexus, with the full momentum generated by your right leg action (Fig. 29) – RUN.

The withdrawal of the leg and kick return is a continuous action taking but a split second to execute in a fluid and powerful movement.

39

Fig. 30

Both wrists held from the front

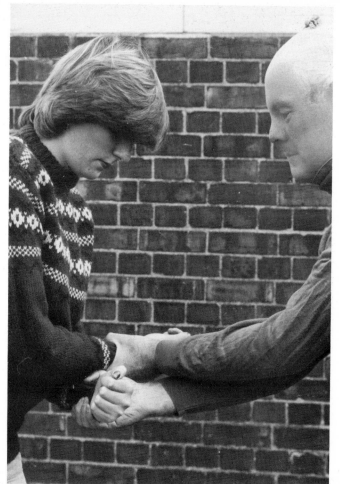

5a.
Your assailant grasps both of your wrists. Act as if to force your hands as far apart as possible (Fig. 30).
(1) Utilising his reaction force to frustrate your movement, bring your hands together as hard as you can – having turned your hands to present the back of one striking the thumb of the other (Fig. 31).
(2) Drive the knee into his groin (Fig. 32). Without pause kick him on the knee and – RUN.

Fig. 31

Fig. 32

5b.
The assailant grasps both of your wrists from the front
(Fig. 33).
(1) Kick the knee, rake the shin and stamp onto his
instep in one continuous movement applying forward
traction against both hands.

Fig. 33

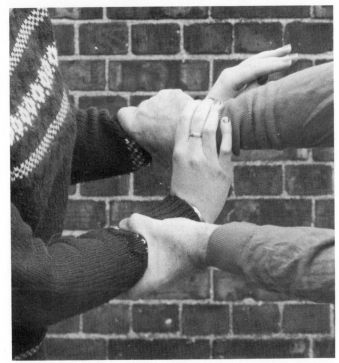

Fig. 34

(2) Immediately grasp the back of the assailant's right hand with your right hand (Fig. 34), and with the combined strength of both arms and the turning of your shoulders to the right, swing his right arm over in a circle until his hand is level with your right hip (Fig. 35). Withdraw your right foot to maintain balance and stable posture.

(3) Keep his wrist 'folded' towards his own elbow and turn his hand clockwise as far as you can, in a forward direction.

(4) Throw your full weight against his extended right elbow joint through the length of your left arm (Fig. 36), your now freed left hand, pressing down onto the top of his arm above the elbow joint. This will throw the assailant onto his face or over in a forward roll – RUN.

Note the position of your own right hand in the illustration.

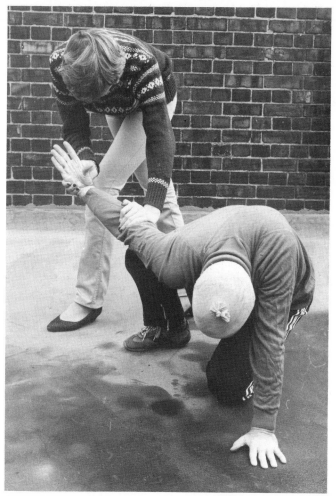

Fig. 35

Fig. 36

One wrist held from the front

6a.
Proceed as in method 5b (2).

6b.
The assailant grasps the right wrist with his right hand.
(1) Immediately kick his knee and without pause swing your left hand hard against the back of his right hand and wrist, and grasp it there.
(2) The momentum and blow will spring your right hand from his grasp (Fig. 37). Maintain your grip at the impact point with your left hand. Without pause swing your right hand back hard against his right wrist which you grasp, and with the combined action of both hands swing his arm upwards in an outward circle (Fig. 38).

Fig. 37

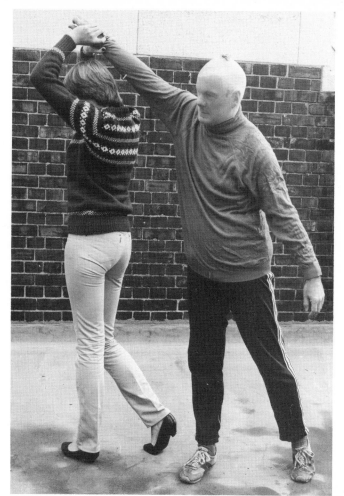

(3) As you do this step forward with your right foot onto the outside of his right foot.

(4) Pivot in one quick clean turn on the balls of your feet so that you now face the same direction as the assailant.

(5) Maintaining momentum and continuous traction using your body weight and the strength of both arms, throw the assailant headlong onto his head.

Note. By retaining the wrist grips taken the momentum of your turn will transmit twist (locking action) on the assailant's right wrist and elbow (Fig. 39), which should be rotated as far as you can twist it in the action.

47

Fig. 38

Fig. 39

Enveloped over the arms from the front

7.

The assailant embraces you over the arms from the front.

(1) Drive your knee into his groin as he closes (Fig. 40), or if the hold is taken, press your right thumb into his left groin – this will create sufficient space between you to consecutively –

(2) Envelop the assailant along the top of his hips with your right arm or lever up under his left armpit and grasp his right arm or sleeve with your left hand near his elbow.

(3) Withdraw your left foot just behind your right and pass your right leg then through between you, placing your right foot on the ground on the 'outside' of his right foot, pointing in the same direction as far as you can place it, without strain or loss of balance (Fig. 41).

Fig. 40

Fig. 41

Enveloped
over the arms
from the front

(4) As your feet are positioned, sink your weight some six inches by bending both knees.

(5) With the concerted action of straightening your legs and turning your body in a rotating circle to your left – lifting with your right arm and pulling with your left hand, the assailant will be lifted off balance onto his toes.

(6) As you turn surge upwards and bend forward from the waist twisting the assailant over your hip. He will be thrown down with some force – RUN.

Note. Keep contact between you and the assailant tightly throughout with your right arm hold. Practice will enable you to precisely place your feet and retain your balance. Balance is the greatest single factor in good technique.

Enveloped under the arms from the front

8.
The assailant tries to embrace you under the arms from the front.
(1) As he closes, drive the knee hard into his groin and with the full force of either hand, drive the heelpalm up in a striking action against his chin (Fig. 42) – RUN. However, the hold may have been secured!

Fig. 42

Enveloped
under the arms
from the front

(2) In this eventuality proceed as follows. Pass your left arm over and encircle his right elbow, reinforcing your hold by grasping the front of his clothing at the left breast (Figs. 43 and 44).

(3) If there is no space to deliver the chin jab as before, drive the right hand's ulna border upwards under his nose, maintain consistent pressure there.

52

Fig. 43

Fig. 44

Enveloped
under the arms
from the front

(4) As the hold around your body is broken, press his head to his right and straighten your left arm retaining your hand hold on his chest. Force both of your arms forward with all your force locking both his arm and neck.

(5) The assailant will be thrown onto his back. If the opportunity is presented as he is forced backwards – strike again with the knee thrust – RUN.

53

Two hands around the throat from the rear

9.

The assailant encircles your throat from the rear with both hands (not his arms).

(1) Grasp his little fingers (only) one in each hand and bend them backwards hard (Fig. 45).

(2) Push your arms outward (Fig. 46) at shoulder

Fig. 45

Fig. 46

Two hands
around the throat
from the rear

height inflicting more pressure on the little finger joints (Fig. 47). Stamp down hard with your right foot driving the heel onto his foot.

(3) Simultaneously – Bring his left arm over your head and cross your own wrists about a foot in front of your right shoulder. As you move your arms drop onto your right knee placing it beside your left foot (not forward) (Fig. 48).

56

Fig. 47

Two hands
around the throat
from the rear

(4) By bending forward from the waist as you drop down and driving both hands forwards and downwards the assailant will be thrown violently forward onto his head – RUN.

Note. To obviate loss of balance to the rear during the action, start bending forward as the hands are moved together as in paragraph (3). The whole action is swift and continuous! Make the movement smooth and do not jerk your arms interrupting the general flow.

Fig. 48

Arm encircles the throat from the rear

10.
The assailant encircles the neck from the rear with his right arm. Act instantly before you are forced over backwards (Fig. 49). Make a vicious chopping cut with the right hand to his groin. This will cause him to bend somewhat forward.

Fig. 49

Fig. 50

Arm encircles
the throat
from the rear

(1) Without pause, bring both hands up and hook them firmly into the crook of his right elbow. Drive the hips back against the assailant (Fig. 50).

(2) In continuous movement, kneel down by dropping
onto your right knee (Fig. 51). Again, kneel near to
your left foot (not forward).
(3) As you drop, bend forward and pull violently with
both hands. This will throw the assailant onto his right
shoulder with considerable force – RUN.

Note. As in all movements, try to avoid preparatory
movements which could give the assailant a lead as to
your intentions!

Fig. 51

Fig. 52

Both arms encircled from the rear

11.
The assailant encircles the arms from the rear by passing his arms around the upper arms with his hands at your back.
(1) Immediately strike your hands backwards against his groin (Fig. 52).

(2) Place the right foot on the ground on the outside of the assailant's right foot and behind the heel (Fig. 53).
(3) Bend and twist your body in conjunction with a movement as if to throw your left arm upwards, and your right arm forward and downward. This rotating action will throw the assailant over your left lower leg, which blocks his right leg movement in attempted recovery of balance – RUN.

Fig. 53

Enveloped
from the rear

12.
The assailant envelopes the arms from the rear by passing his arms around you and joining his hands in front of you.
(1) Take a deep breath and force your arms outward as far as you can against this hold (Fig. 54). It will be fractional! Join your hands together to reinforce your action.

Fig. 54

(2) Now exhale and drop your weight sufficiently to place both hands on the assailants right arm as near his elbow as you can. Grasp the arm or clothing there.
(3) Put your right leg back on the outside of his right leg as far as you can, your inside right knee against his outer right knee (Fig. 55).
(4) Rotate quickly bringing his weight against your right leg which is now straightened rapidly acting as a spring to throw him headlong over your leg – RUN.

Note. If the assailant, having encircled your body lifts you bodily from the ground – all is not lost! Throw both legs straight out in front of you at waist height. This sudden change of balance will cause the assailant to bend forward. As your feet return to the ground, let the right leg continue to the previous spring throwing position. Act as before and roll him to the ground – RUN.

Fig. 55

Encircled under the arms from the rear

13.
The assailant encircles you under the arms joining his hands at your waist.
(1) Grasp your own wrist so that your forearms form one straight line. Drive the right elbow back against the right temple of the assailant with the full swing of your shoulders reinforced by both arms (Fig. 56). Without pause, and timed to catch him rebounding to the left, drive your left elbow back in a scything action against his left temple. This should be a fast rocking action. Should it be necessary, then proceed as follows.

Fig. 56

Encircled
under the arms
from the rear

(2) Shift your weight and balance onto your left leg.
(3) Pass your right leg backwards and hook the back of
the assailant's right ankle with your right foot, from
the outside (Fig. 57). Bend forward a little as you do
this to bring the assailants weight onto his toes. With
practice onto his left toes.
(4) Now sweep his right leg forward in a slightly
outward circular movement and sit your weight (drop)
onto his extended knee joint. He will fall away onto his
back with a wrenched knee – RUN.

Fig. 57

Both wrists held from the rear

14.
The assailant grasps both of your wrists from the rear.
(1) Immediately kick the heel backwards into the groin
(Fig. 58), or depending on opportunity and distance,
stamp your heel hard onto his foot.
(2) Utilising this diversionary action carry out the
following actions concurrently and speedily in a
sweeping movement.

Fig. 58

(3) Bring your hands up passing your left hand over your head grasping the assailant's right wrist, maintaining forward traction meanwhile.

(4) Lowering your body as you do this (Fig. 60), to obviate being overbalanced backwards, drop quickly onto your right knee as you did in method 9. With the momentum created, and the forward and downward thrust of both arms, the assailant will be thrown heavily forward – RUN.

Note. As with all 'major movement methods' there must be no break between the elements of the actions, or grips released (Fig. 59). All the sections must flow as one fluid action sequence!

Fig. 59

Fig. 60

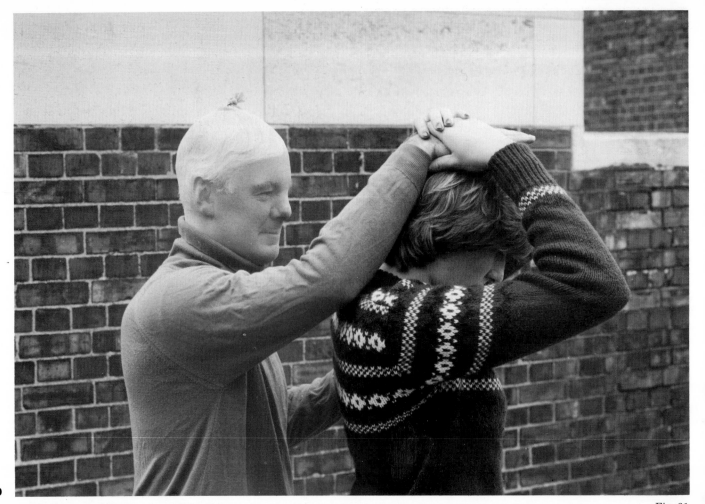

Fig. 61

Held by the hair from the rear

15.
The assailant holds your hair from the rear with his right hand (Fig. 61). Before he can pull you backwards act as follows.
(1) Immediately grasp his wrist with both hands and by crossing your right foot over your left, pivot to face him.
(2) His hand should be kept as tight as possible against your head so that if you turn and lean away from him, you will lock his wrist and strain it (Fig. 62).
(3) Without pause, as the turn is completed and he is stretched upwards by the pressure on his wrist, kick him as hard as you can in the groin (Fig. 62) – RUN.

Fig. 62

Fig. 63

Held down on the ground — attacker in astride position

16.
You are on your back on the ground and the assailant straddles your body with a knee on each side of your waist (Fig. 63). His hands pin your wrists to the ground. (This position stabilises his posture as his weight can be readily shifted to bring pressure onto either wrist at will, to frustrate your struggles).
(1) Suddenly without warning put all your power into your right arm in an attempt to push it upwards. Clearly you will be unable to do this! However your purpose has been served. The assailant will swing his weight automatically in that direction to pin that arm more firmly. This will reduce the weight on your left arm.

Fig. 64

(2) Shoot your left arm along the ground straight above your head (Fig. 64). Now roll to the left using your right hand push and body roll (Fig. 65) to roll him off. You will be surprised how well this works! Get up and – RUN.

Fig. 65

17.
The assailant kneels between your knees and is holding you down (Fig. 66). If you cannot proceed as before, carry out the following.

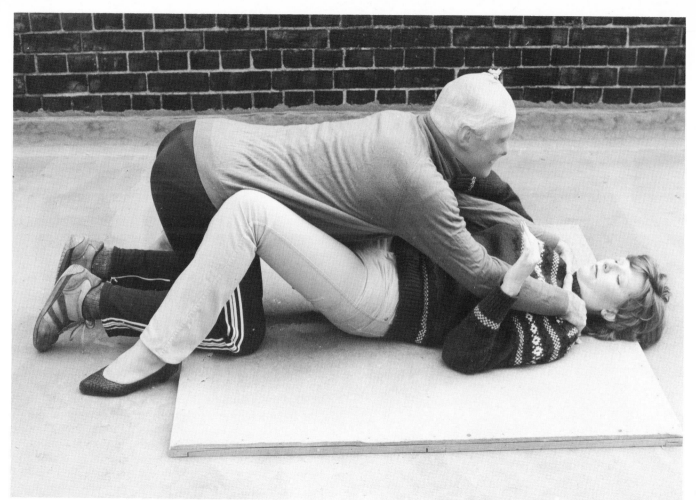

Fig. 66

Held on the ground
in the 'rape' position

(1) Pass your legs over his legs and between them, your heels coming together. Without pause hook your feet under his ankles (Fig. 67).
(2) Drive the legs straight out. This will lock his thighs in a most painful manner and he will be pinned.
(3) Grasp his collar by inserting the fingers on each side of his neck, pulling your hands towards you, and with the lever on his collar, drive the knuckles of each hand hard into his neck just behind the 'Adam's apple'. SHOUT for help.

Note. If the assailant 'passes out' (which is extremely likely) roll him off and – RUN.

Fig. 67

Published in Great Britain by
Kay & Ward Ltd
The Windmill Press, Kingswood, Tadworth, Surrey

Printed in Great Britain by
Biddles Ltd, Guildford and King's Lynn

ISBN 0 7182 2970 3